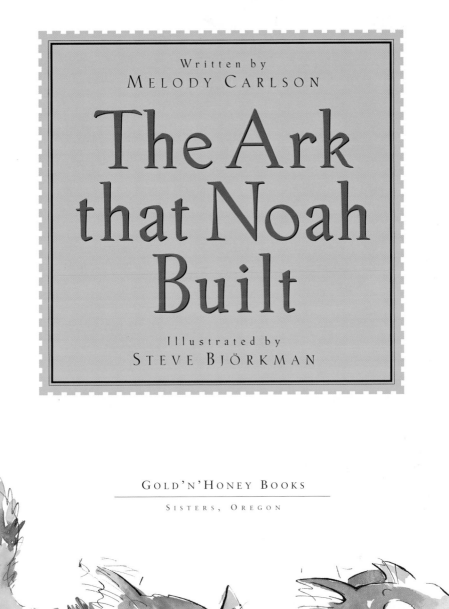

Written by
MELODY CARLSON

The Ark that Noah Built

Illustrated by
STEVE BJÖRKMAN

GOLD'N'HONEY BOOKS

SISTERS, OREGON

MC JY CP

The Ark That Noah Built

published by Gold'n'Honey Books
a part of the Questar publishing family

© 1997 by Questar Publishers, Inc.

International Standard Book Number:1-57673-058-1

Illustrations © 1997 by Steve Bjorkman

Text by Melody Carlson

Design by D2 DesignWorks

Printed in Hong Kong

For information:
QUESTAR PUBLISHERS, INC.
POST OFFICE BOX 1720
SISTERS, OREGON 97759

Library of Congress Cataloging-in-Publication Data:

97 98 99 00 01 — 10 9 8 7 6 5 4 3 2

To Bridget, Robert, Ryan, and Amanda
— M. C.

To Jennifer, Robert, Steven, and Daniel Moody
— S. B.

This is the ark that Noah built.

This is the grain

that was stored in the ark that Noah built.

These are the rats that nibbled the grain that was stored in the ark that Noah built.

And these are the cats

that chased the rats, that nibbled the grain

that was stored in the ark that Noah built.

These are the dogs that growled at the cats, that chased the rats, that nibbled the grain, that was stored in the ark that Noah built.

These are the tigers with razor-sharp claws, that frightened the dogs that growled at the cats, that chased the rats, that nibbled the grain that was stored in the ark that Noah built.

These are the alligators with wide-open jaws, that snapped at the tigers with razor-sharp claws, that frightened the dogs, that growled at the cats, that chased the rats, that nibbled the grain that was stored in the ark that Noah built.

These are the monkeys

with shrieking cries, that teased the alligators

with wide-open jaws, that snapped at the

tigers with razor-sharp claws, that frightened

the dogs, that growled at the cats, that chased

the rats, that nibbled the grain that was

stored in the ark that Noah built.

These are the snakes with hypnotic eyes, that charmed the monkeys with shrieking cries, that teased the alligators with wide-open jaws, that snapped at the tigers with razor-sharp claws, that frightened the dogs, that growled at the cats, that chased the rats, that nibbled the grain that was stored in the ark that Noah built.

These are the elephants

with the stomping feet, that scattered the snakes

with hypnotic eyes, that charmed the monkeys

with shrieking cries, that teased the alligators

with wide-open jaws, that snapped at the tigers

with razor-sharp claws, that frightened the

dogs, that growled at the cats, that chased the

rats, that nibbled the grain that was stored in

the ark that Noah built.

These are the bees

that were robbed of their treat, that stung

the elephants with the stomping feet, that

scattered the snakes with hypnotic eyes, that

charmed the monkeys with shrieking cries,

that teased the alligators with wide-open jaws,

that snapped at the tigers with razor-sharp

claws, that frightened the dogs, that growled

at the cats, that chased the rats, that nibbled

the grain that was stored in the ark that

Noah built.

These are the bears that ate all the honey, that angered the bees that were robbed of their treat, that stung the elephants with the stomping feet, that scattered the snakes with hypnotic eyes, that charmed the monkeys with shrieking cries, that teased the alligators with wide-open jaws, that snapped at the tigers with razor-sharp claws, that frightened the dogs, that growled at the cats, that chased the rats, that nibbled the grain that was stored in the ark that Noah built.

These are the hyenas

that thought it was funny, that laughed at the bears that ate all the honey, that angered the bees that were robbed of their treat, that stung the elephants with the stomping feet, that scattered the snakes with hypnotic eyes, that charmed the monkeys with shrieking cries, that teased the alligators with wide-open jaws, that snapped at the tigers with razor-sharp claws, that frightened the dogs, that growled at the cats, that chased the rats, that nibbled the grain that was stored in the ark that Noah built.

"What is going on down here?"

This is Noah who yelled

so loud, who quieted the hyenas that thought it was funny, that laughed at the bears that ate all the honey, that angered the bees that were robbed of their treat, that stung the elephants with the stomping feet, that scattered the snakes with their hypnotic eyes, that charmed the monkeys with shrieking cries, that teased the alligators with wide-open jaws, that snapped at the tigers with razor-sharp claws, that frightened the dogs, that growled at the cats, that chased the rats, that nibbled the grain that was stored in the ark that Noah built.

This is the dove that broke

through the cloud, sent by Noah who yelled so loud, who quieted the hyenas that thought it was funny, that laughed at the bears that ate all the honey, that angered the bees that were robbed of their treat, that stung the elephants with the stomping feet, that scattered the snakes with their hypnotic eyes, that charmed the monkeys with shrieking cries, that teased the alligators with wide-open jaws, that snapped at the tigers with razor-sharp claws, that frightened the dogs, that worried the cats, that chased the rats, that nibbled the grain that was stored in the ark that Noah built.

And this is God's promise to you and to me

Written by rainbow and twig of a tree

A promise to lead us and guide us always

To love and protect us the rest of our days.